# Jewish Mindfulness for Kids

To the loves of my life - Miguel, my partner in life and greatest teammate, and Jonathan, Galit and Orly, my loving kids and best teachers. —B.S.

To Luna, my little flower —C.C.

KAR-BEN PUBLISHING®
An imprint of Lerner Publishing Group, Inc.
241 First Avenue North
Minneapolis, MN 55401 USA

Website address: www.karben.com

Main body text set in Mikado Regular.
Typeface provided by HVD Fonts.

**Library of Congress Cataloging-in-Publication Data**

Names: Sissa, Blanca, author. | Carrossine, Camila, illustrator.
Title: Jewish mindfulness for kids / by Blanca Sissa ; illustrated by Camila Carrossine.
Description: Minneapolis, MN : Kar-Ben Publishing, [2024] | Audience: Ages 3-8 | Audience: Grades K-1 | Summary: "The exercises in this unique book encourage children to use every-day items to inspire mindfulness. Mindfulness, the Jewish value of Yishuv Hada'at, means paying attention to what is happening around us"– Provided by publisher.
Identifiers: LCCN 2023004417 (print) | LCCN 2023004418 (ebook) | ISBN 9781728486444 (library binding) | ISBN 9798765613436 (epub)
Subjects: LCSH: Mindfulness–Religious aspects–Judaism–Juvenile literature.
Classification: LCC BM645.M56 S57 2024 (print) | LCC BM645.M56 (ebook) | DDC 158.1/3–dc23/eng/20230504

LC record available at https://lccn.loc.gov/2023004417
LC ebook record available at https://lccn.loc.gov/2023004418

Manufactured in China
1-52562-50754-4/18/2023

# Jewish Mindfulness for Kids

Blanca Sissa

illustrated by Camila Carrossine

KAR-BEN
PUBLISHING

Our mind is like a forest of many trees.
A lot of jumping monkeys arrive.
The monkeys are our thoughts.
They jump wildly from branch to branch.
Our mind follows the jumping. Our mind does not sit still.
Suddenly, we are thinking of a friend we saw yesterday,
a favorite TV show,
Bubbe's cookies.

Our mind gets tired
from chasing all the monkeys.
Let's help our mind sit and rest,
in the here and now.
That's called **mindfulness**.

Mindfulness is part of the Jewish tradition.
We call it **Yishuv Hada'at**.
Concentration.
Paying attention to what is happening around us.
Here and now.

We are not sad about something that happened yesterday.
We do not worry about something that might happen tomorrow.
We focus on this special moment.
We breathe.
We listen to the sounds around us.

Little by little, during the day,
we take moments to rest our body
and our mind.
We think of only one thing: our **breathing**.

We breathe in.
And out.

When we breathe like this, we calm down.
The monkeys go quiet and still
For just a little while.

Afterward, our mind feels stronger,
ready to learn more,
come up with great ideas,
and have fun.

Now that we know how important it is to breathe
and how much it helps us,
let's learn some fun ways to breathe!

## Challah and Chicken Soup

Let's imagine that in one hand,
we have a piece of fresh challah.
It smells so good!

In the other hand, we have a
spoonful of hot chicken soup.
It's very, very hot!

Let's smell our challah.
Let's take a breath.

We want to eat our hot chicken soup,
but we have to cool it down.

Let's blow on the chicken soup.
Let's let our breath out slowly.
We smell the challah.
We blow on the hot chicken soup.

## Blow the Shofar

Let's pretend it's Yom Kippur
and we get to blow the shofar.

First, we breathe in.
Next, we blow into our pretend shofar.
Again.

We breathe in.
We blow the shofar.

And once more.
In our mind, we hear the blast of the shofar.

## Be a Dove

Let's be peaceful like a dove.
We will fly soon, but not just yet.

We breathe in air and extend our wings.

We let the air out very slowly.
And repeat.

## Wander through the Desert

The Jewish people left slavery in Egypt
and wandered in the desert for forty years.
So we are very good at wandering slowly.

Let's "take a walk" through our body. We pretend
we are a dune in the desert. We kneel on the floor.
Sitting back on our heels, we slowly bring our head
down to rest on the floor. We relax and breathe.

First, we pay attention to our legs.
We notice their position. We let them lie still.

Next, we think about the center of our body.
We notice how the tummy rises
and falls
to the rhythm of our breathing.

We pay attention to our chest.
We notice our breath
and the way our heart is beating.

We notice our arms and hands.
Our arms lie loosely at the sides of our body,
and our hands are still.

Now we pay attention to our face.
Our jaw is relaxed.
Our eyes are closed.
We release our breath very slowly.

We open our eyes.
We have reached our destination.
We are in the Land of Israel!

# Light the Shabbat Candles

Shabbat candlelight is special.

Once the candles are lit,
let's quietly look at them for a little while.

We breathe in and out as the candle flames flicker,
watching as they point toward the sky.
The candlelight never stops changing.
Neither do we.

Shalom

Shalom

Shalom

## Sing Shalom

We are going to meditate with a special word. Let's focus on the sound of the word *shalom*, which means "peace."

We close our eyes.
We slowly say the word *shalom* three times.
*Shaaaaa lommmmm . . .*

We stretch out the sound of the word.
*Shaaaaa lommmmm . . . Shaaaaa lommmmm . . .*

We say the word *shalom* three more times.
*Shalom. Shalom. Shalom.*

We open our eyes.
We are ready for the rest of our day.

We enjoy the beauty of the world.

## Author's Note

Staying quiet can be one of the hardest things for kids to do. Breathing is a simple and effective tool to help them calm themselves. With these exercises, kids learn to relax their bodies and to lower their energy levels. They learn to have moments of calm.

*Yishuv Hada'at* makes children aware of their own bodies, helps them connect emotions and thoughts, and encourages concentration, memory, and emotional validation.

Children live in a hurried and sometimes stressful world. Studies show that mindfulness practices can ease anxiety, depression, and stress while helping kids learn to self-regulate and to pay attention to their bodies. The exercises in this book will introduce kids to healthy habits that they can build on throughout their lives.

## About the Author

Blanca Sissa is a certified kids' yoga instructor and teacher trainer in yoga resources for the classroom. Originally from México City, Mexico, she lives in Madrid, Spain.

## About the Illustrator

Camila Carrossine was born and lives in São Paulo, Brazil. She has been drawing since she was a little girl, first on her bedroom walls and today on the pages of books. She has illustrated more than fifty books.

*Scan the QR code to watch author and yoga master Blanca Sissa lead you through Jewish Mindfulness exercises!*